Medium of the Breath

Medium of the Breath

Dharma Poems for Here and Now

Richard Arthure

Copyright © 2010 by Richard Arthure.

ISBN:		Softcover		978-1-4535-3009-2

All rights reserved. No part of this book may be reproduced or transmitted in any form or by any means, electronic or mechanical, including photocopying, recording, or by any information storage and retrieval system, without permission in writing from the copyright owner.

This book was printed in the United States of America.

To order additional copies of this book, contact:
Xlibris Corporation
1-888-795-4274
www.Xlibris.com
Orders@Xlibris.com
83410

Contents

Medium of the breath—tonglen tango 7

Dragonfly Gift 9

Hotel Vajra 11

Haiku 13

Lonely Promises 14

Pizza Wars 16

Remembering the kind root guru Chokyi Gyatso
   the 11th Trungpa Tulku 17

The Day My Mother Died 19

Widely Scattered Showers 21

How High Full Moon 22

Fire 23

Convergence 24

But What of the Light Side? 26

Celebrating Sybil Liverties 28

Gentil Livre, écoutez! 30

Dear Notebook, listen to me! 31

Don't rain on my tirade 32

Gratitude 36

Kyoto in Autumn 38

La Grande Illusion 39

Louisiana Party Pick-Up 41

Dog Day Blues 42

No Regret 43

What if I take the Jewel Lake pills? 45

Summer Lightning 49

Song of Dependent Origination..................................... 51

Sunshine Angel 53

Nothing Wanting.. 55

Magnetic 58

Doubtful Katheryn 59

Beaucoup Haiku for Katie Sue 61

Sonnetry confinement 62

Zozobra.. 63

The white page is an invitation 64

Song for Dakini Kate 66

Resolution... 67

Storm before the war 68

The Blessed of my life 70

Them Apples 72

Things to Remember 74

The elephants in your wallet 76

Book summary 77

About the Author 79

Medium of the breath—tonglen tango

Alright, I'll write, not words reflected on
but starbursts of radiant light from nowhere, the deepest inner space.
It's neither here nor there, it's everywhere, its messenger the bright green hummingbird with scarlet throat sipping from red geranium flowers sunlit
shivering warmly in summer breeze outside this cabin on Greenhorn Mountain
as joy percolates exhales bubble up sizzles from fingertips through neurons to blue jays and small lizards
(why oh why those tiny ants love to gather and sing songs in the scallop shell I put used teabags in?)
and out, out, out to foxes chipmunks bears turkeys marmots deer and chipmunks,
all human and non-human beings in Orphan Valley and beyond,
New Mexico—please dance and play guitarras, tap feet, strike drums in every pueblo
and share the pulsing rhythm of happiness without reason in bustling cities Albuquerque Phoenix Denver Chicago The Angels of California Saint Francisco
may this vibrant joy be yours to wiggle your toes and ease your woes that no-one knows this blood's for you!

Just give me in return—address unknown return to sender—
yr skull-cracking anxieties hypertension yr hot black misery stomach-cramping hunger yr impotent murderous purple rage
yr long-held grievances irritations beyond the reach of Excedrin and Valium and extra strength Tylenol
yr headaches ulcers and joint-twisting arthritic inflammations,
yr gasping for breath emphysema and cancerous agonies of toxic self hate
give me yr jailhouse blues head-hanging disappointments and suicide despairs: I drink them in.
I take upon me yr muffled sorrow nightmare fears cockroach tenement Snoop dog-eat-dog murder rape barroom and crack house round and round addictions, *khorwa,*

yr hunched and stooped depression salt tears of self-pity and remorse
all the pain of wasted life twisted limbs I breathe it in.
I draw it in hot and sulphurous through every pore deep down into the
core of my being, there's room for more.

And again I radiate and offer you in the ten directions
cool and blissful all-joy luminous peace nothing wanting
like a gentle summer rain that quenches every thirst and out of nowhere
brings an unexpected smile
refreshing breeze of deep contentment sending and gathering
gathering and sending on the medium of the breath
sending and gathering for all beings everywhere.

Dragonfly Gift

Twelve times or more the dragonfly
landed on the back of my right hand,
opened and closed transparent wings
reflecting rainbow colors,
groomed itself fastidiously,
summoned two more of its kind
and they settled, one on either side
of my visitor, while the sunflower nodded,
a scarlet-breasted linnet looked on
and purposeful consciousness fell away
like a silk bedspread slipping to the floor.

Why do you bring me
this brief gift of sleep
on a summer afternoon?
Is it to remind me of other gifts,
of other visitors in the drowsy
dream time twixt asleep and wake?

I dreamt that Kayla Moonwatcher
was uncertain whether she could ride
a certain powerful stallion,
yet mounted him and rode
with graceful and triumphant ease
while a policeman on a pony
pursued her impotently,
was thrust against an iron fence
and thrown from his mount,
his left leg crushed as the pony
fell on him in slow motion.

I awoke from a reverie this morning
and remembered being barefoot
inside the engine of a motorcycle.
There was straw on the floor

and bits of barbed wire and
a huge rusty pipe rose vertically.
An older, wiser man
was repairing the bike
and trying to teach me zen
and the Art of Motorcycle Maintenance,
but I was more interested in
drying off my wet and muddy feet
and reflecting that
I only rode the bike anyway
for the sake of a girl.

Now in my yard the shadows
are creeping up on me
and I'm too lazy
to move the chaise longue.
The dragonfly is gone
leaving only the faint
remembered imprint
on the back of my hand
of six delicate feet
poised for flight.
It must be time to go inside
and cook the dinner.

Hotel Vajra

Pigeons flowing playful
on wind currents
my yellow umbrella neatly furled
no place to go
just Pagoda Bar
on rooftop of Vajra Hotel

pigeon friends inquisitive
cock their heads and look at us
iridescent turquoise neck feathers
gleaming slick
maybe they'd like some apple pie
Todd liked it
now he's reading *Billy Budd*

bamboo waves easy in the big wind
bamboo Billy Budd
seven years before the mast
and never could figure out the—
Darn! That pigeon's peering at me again
just can't mind his own business

and I'm just bamboo billy budding here
as rain stops
trees all shiny
Kathmandu valley holds its breath
mind stops
just a gap
many times repeated
what-it-is-actually
no-one here seeing it

just cock the head
and gaze up at it
bamboo sky
billy budding
now
and now
and again now

As rain stops
mind stops
then gentle even flow
Even Point
apple Pie
American as maybe
as Tibetan as momos
as vast as this Nepali sky

Haiku

stainless steel saucepan lid
shaving each morning
you are my faithful mirror

snow covering the mountainside
after finished the dishes
there'll be time to watch it falling

toilet paper shredded
wonder why that chipmunk
is building its nest in the outhouse?

instead of doing the laundry
I'll sit on a red zafu
and watch my thoughts go round and round

meditating on emptiness
spilled tea on the zabutan
cup not as empty as I'd thought

fat cloud floating up there
just too damn lazy
to write a poem

Lonely Promises

Christmas—calling my son Michael and his mother
intercepts the call, hangs up—and it ain't that easy
to even get a line to Toronto December 25th.
Good to be lonely on Christmas Day, naturally
the loneliest day of the year and grateful to the Guru
as matchmaker, marrying me to this place of solitude.
But how the hell can I write this lonely blues when
crazy gray cat with green eyes is chewing on the end of my pen?
Need someone to play with?
How about a cotton mouse with a red tail? There you go . . .
and leave me play with my empty stuffing thoughts
flavored with fresh rosemary, thyme and white sage,
while the chicken roasts in the oven and I see the end of life
drawing near like a river running to the sea.

Oh, death, my own death, surest of companions,
walk behind me a little longer before I finish
this sweet life's journey. Isn't it time to look towards
those end-games, completion activities,
if-it-isn't-done-soon-it-never-will-be-things? My heart does long to embrace
the loneliness of retreat, following the example of the father Gurus,
Tulku Urgyen especially. Hard to think of him without tears of longing.
Hard to remember his face of unutterable kindness
without knowing in the marrow of my bones
I made a promise. I promised you—I will do as much retreat practice as
the circumstances of my life permit.
And you said, *Thujeche, thujeche*. Thank you, thank you.
I can hear your voice right now. Like a salmon
I twist and swim and leap upstream to that moment
in the river of my life that forever changed its course.

I am an ungrateful ass, I admit it.
But when I remember you, I do feel
the deepest gratitude; I do remember my promise.
I hold dear the precious teachings you gave me.
I recognized mind nature—however briefly—
and your words struck home. You said—
*If a man's life is compared to the twenty-four hour
cycle of a day, in your life it's already past midnight.
Isn't it time to devote yourself to Dharma practice?*

My 59th birthday is less than a month away.
If I don't practice with diligence now,
won't I feel regret at the time of death?
And who knows when death will catch up with me
and this life will end?
Looking into mind again and again—
is there something more important than this?

I confess to being attached to every kind of distraction,
to all that takes me away from the oh-so-subtle love affair
with glorious solitude, the yogin's friend. Somehow
I shall remember my promise. And keep it too.
Else I am a traitorous wretch. And that's the truth.

Pizza Wars

Pepperoni bullets,
mozzarella missiles:
it's the pizza wars.

Denigrating each other,
screaming at the children:
it's marital mayhem.

Competing for attention,
teasing the youngest:
it's fraternal rivalry.

Feeling inadequate,
blaming your partner:
it's domestic disharmony.

Paying lip serving to the Dharma
while cultivating superior aggression:
it's spiritual suicide.

Knowing the problem will be solved
if your partner would only change:
this is self-deception.

Cutting the commission
to make another deal:
this is not generosity.

Struggling frantically
in the net of hope and fear:
this is not freedom.

Seeing all these
is not quite the same
as treading on the Path,

But perhaps it's a start . . .

Remembering the kind root guru Chokyi Gyatso the 11ᵗʰ TrungpaTulku

Why am I crying into bacon and eggs at Lickskillet Café?
Because it's Shambhala Day and I should be with my Dharma brothers and sisters;
Because I found you, Chogyam Trungpa, Chokyi Gyastso, 30 years ago
And when I went to meet you at Biddulph you knew I was coming, though I had told no-one where I was going;
Because you saw right through me and punched me on the nose to wake me up when I needed it;
Because you named me Kunga Dawa, All-Joyful Moon, and I never suffered from depression again;
Because when I was losing my mind you promised I would never escape from you and I never could;
Because you pointed out ordinary mind when I least expected it and said "Welcome to the circle,"
Because you gave me Maha Ati teaching so casually it took 25 years to realize how rare and precious the oral instructions;
Because you entered me into the path of the profound mantrayana and gave my life meaning it never had before;
Because you took me to India, Bhutan and Sikkim and empowered me with Dorje Trollo Karma Pakshi, wrathful embodiment of crazy wisdom;
Because you told me I could actually attain enlightenment in this very lifetime and I believed you;
Because I swore an oath of allegiance and now there is no turning back;
Because you told me in New Delhi there would be a rainbow in the sky at your cremation and 20 years later I lived to see it;
Because you were completely outrageous and inscrutable, your realization vast as the sky, and the ignorant saw only a drunken womanizer;
Because you could read my mind always and there was no place to hide;
Because I was naked and exposed every time I saw you or thought of you and still am;
Because I had an out-of-body experience on acid and you alone were able to bring me back;

Because you never gave up on me even though I was your most obstinate student;
Because you once despaired of being able to bring the Dharma to the West and took too many sleeping pills and we nearly lost you;
Because you gave all your money to an old beggar woman in Bodhgaya and your girlfriend got angry at you;
Because your mother-in-law hated you, called you nigger, swore she would crush you under foot like a cockroach
And you transformed vituperative South African farmer's daughter into dignified lovable genteel Lady Pybus;
Because the geese are honking in the crystal winter sky and I know you are laughing at some cosmic joke;
Because if it wasn't for you I wouldn't be here, and I wouldn't want to be anywhere else.

I supplicate space, Chokyi Gyatso,
Inseparable space and awareness, Chokyi Gyatso,
Bliss and emptiness, Chokyi Gyatso,
Lord of the realm of non-thought, Chokyi Gyatso.
Please look on your heart-son with compassion, Chokyi Gyatso.
Grant your blessing so that I may always remember you with devotion,
Grant your blessing so that I will practice the Dharma with unwavering diligence,
Grant your blessing so that the seeds you planted may ripen and blossom into realization.

Chokyi Gyatso, Chokyi Gyatso, Ocean of Dharma, I'm drowning, I'm drowning, I can taste the salt of you right now,
Trickling down cheek, flavoring eggs at Lickskillet Café.
And the waitress is looking at me kind of funny.
"Are you alright?" she's asking me.
Yes. Yes, I'm fine, I'm fine. Everything is fine, thank you.

The Day My Mother Died

The day my mother died
there was a lunar eclipse.
The phone rang at 4 am,
I sat up quickly,
knew *something* must have happened.
My sister's voice was saying:
"mummy died an hour ago,
it happened quickly.
I saw her eyes roll
and called an ambulance.
It was a ruptured aneurism."

I could hear my father sobbing
ten thousand miles away
right inside my head.
A dead calm surrounded me,
not a breath of emotional prana wind.
And again the distance meant nothing,
the mind knows no limitations
except those it chooses.

In my mind's eye I see her,
Dickie Arthure right in front of me
stretched out on a hospital bed,
above her, Guru Rinpoche.
In a blaze of dazzling light,
ten million mega watts
of wisdom radiance pure compassion
shine from the Guru's heart,
illuminate and bathe her body
penetrating every cell.
My mother's mind essence,
a sphere of white light,
shoots out through the crown of her head,
is absorbed into the Guru's heart center.

My darling mother,
whether you reincarnate
or not is up to you.
Day break comes,
I sleep briefly.
In my dream
I'm in the room
with my sister Frances
and my father.
He is sobbing.
The phone rings,
Frances answers,
holds out the phone to me:
"it's for you."
Mummy is speaking,
tells me Elaine is coming to the house,
chatters on sweetly
to my astonishment.
Finally I have to ask:
"Is it really possible
you are not dead after all?"
Dead silence
then the line is disconnected.
I wake with the memory of this
the day my mother died.

Widely Scattered Showers

Lilacs at the bottom of my garden tap me on the nose.
The irises are sticking out their magenta tongues
like twenty-seven Mick Jaggers lollygagging against the fence.
Red and yellow tulips are taunting the mule deer
that gather along goose creek—"Come and get it!"
From high up in the old cottonwood tree
blue jay dive bombs a crow
and—watch out—here she comes again
missing mister Crow by inches.
Dang, that was close! What has she got against him, I wonder?
Meanwhile this chaise longue supports my scrawny body
as the mower stands idle in the long grass.
I'm sure it's me, not it, that has run out of gas.
But soon I'll remember why I'm here,
the sacred purpose of life
and I'll be galvanized into timeless inaction
floating on a sea of crickets.
Now raindrops getting fat and greasy.
Instead of mowing the lawn, perhaps
I should go for a haircut. Truth to say, though,
I rather like having long hair, not working a regular job,
leading the lonely life of a poet and yogin.
I am resolved; I'll stay awhile under this apple tree
craving union with the bliss-bestowing consort of my mind
fangs bared, ready to slice and dice with her gleaming hooked knife.
I'll cut my loved one's initials in the damp grass
and erase them forever from the lush green tablet of my yard.
Vrmmmmmmmmh vrmmmmmmmmmh power mower sounds like
old ferry boat chugging across the harbor from Halifax to Dartmouth,
a clutch of commuters huddled in the bow
smoking cigarettes and dreaming of a warm supper.
Don't you love those widely scattered showers in Spring?

How High Full Moon

Full moon rising of over Sangre de Cristos
Young man seeing three moons through honeycomb
Lenses, the pinprick obstruction to perfect vision,
Taste of bud brownies to the sound of jazz
Bird and Diz soaring higher than moon itself
Dropping from it fertile shit seeds to sprout
On New Mexico mountain highlands
Looking down and up above green Tara's
Merciful compassion for weed-craving youths
Hiking through sky in search of lava soil
From ancient volcanoes now asleep.
No more eruptions just interruptions
Resolved at last in this perfect blue chord.

Note: How High Full Moon is a collaborative poem written by Richard Arthure and Michael Arthure, writing alternate lines.

Fire

Fire, fire, fire, fire, fire,
without you we would freeze,
before you came we could not see.
Now you are here,
now I embrace you
now I'm cooking
hot spicy food
crackling in the pan.
Fire that nourishes,
you turn dead meat
into juicy steak,
you turn cold fish
into passionate lover.
Embraceable you,
sweet fire
adorable flame
consuming hesitation
kindling the vivid interchange
between the knower and the known:
whatever you lick
with your tricky flickering tongue
is utterly devoured.
Making love with you
is so fiercely final.
Toes tingle and burst into flame,
my knees and thighs ignite,
fiery arms embrace me
amber flesh to flashing embers.
Farewell world. Fire, I'm yours.

Convergence

Poetry is heart's vibrant yearning
expressed in sound.
Wine is sunlight
held together by water
from the ground.
Bread is wheat leavened
by yeasty fungal fission.
Butter is cow's milk
beaten into gold submission.
Mind is continuity
of change without remission.

How did the coming together
 of you, my dear, and me
converge in unexpected harmony?
I have no answer.
I stepped from the little Cessna
at Lebanon, New Hampshire,
and the sight of you, sky dancer,
tall, blue-eyed, rosy cheeked,
struck a major chord
in the key of *now-I-see*.
Looking in each other's eyes,
there was no separate me:
conjoining what's below and what's above,
the tone vibration of equality and love.

Four weeks have passed
and now you're far away.
Impermanence alone
is here to stay.
The man I thought I was
has vanished without trace.
You touched that seeming solid me
and it dissolved in space.

But still I live and love and choose
to sing now with a softer voice
in a minor key, a gentler blues,
because I have no choice.
I'll celebrate the shifting sands,
the way the tide will come and go,
remembering how mind expands
when all I'm doing is letting go.
There's nothing to hold onto anyway
and, knowing this, I sing my soft hooray!

But What of the Light Side?

Ragged flag flops loosely
like a worn out harlequin.
Beyond, a dozen small birds peck
at the dry cold stony ground.
What nutrients they find there
is an avian mystery.
A lone magpie glides down
waddles a few steps.
The steep hillside is stamped with perfect snow
and an army of straight tall pines
stands guard over the valley.

In here, the snort and sneeze and cough
erupt to pierce the silent ruminations
of meditators, their jackhammer
thoughts pounding in their patient skulls.
Sonia's femur is healing slowly,
the brave and feisty girl,
a mere two weeks since she dropped the crutches;
and the FEMA that failed us
when New Orleans was shattered
by wind and sea will maybe never end.

The oil-addicted neocons
are plotting their next insane war.
"We must go to the dark side"
Dick Cheney has declared.
But what of the light side?
The brilliant sunlight of open heart,
warrior bravery? Is it up to us?
Are we up to it?
Going out with the breath again and again,

liberating one by one
the chain of crazy thoughts.
A glimpse of sanity and ready
to reach out to the starving world?
The combo of love affair and loneliness:
is this what we have to offer?
Just our warm heart's blood
and willing to let go, now and now
and embrace the unknown stranger
with her wild hair and staring eyes?
Let it be so!

Celebrating Sybil Liverties

In pitch dark
moon not yet risen
sparkling dots of light
appear, coalesce
in luminous patterns.

starfish collide exquisitely
in galactic dance
neutrons and protons
whiz around at top speed
bearing timely messages

photons exult piercing
the seeming solid
in wave after wave
thoughts are stubbed out
on the rock of unwavering
mind leaving nothing
but a shower of sparks behind

ting-a-ling ting-a-ling
timeless bells resound
in empty skull drum
summoning dakinis
white sky dancers
make their presence felt
invisibly on the inbreath

their laughter echoing
in bone mirror corridors
and neural pathways
percolating up
through cerebrum
to night sky cosmic
stardust bliss pavilions

Good things are happening
on planet earth along
the tingling spine
of America where
mountain hot springs
bubble up unlicensed
and celebrants bathe naked
and freely speak their minds
undeterred by Bushcroft's icy hand
tightening the noose
on Sybil's lovely vive la liberte.

Gentil Livre, écoutez!

Il faut que je dise,
rien que pour voir ou ça mène,
des choses qui ne troublent personne.

Nuit humide. Enfants couchés.
Grâce à l'absence des critiques sévères,
j'ose parler. Je me souviens, d'abord,
d'une chose frappante :
je me réjouis d'elle en ce moment même.
Oui, solitude précieuse, c'est bien de toi
que je parle, et puis il faut bien
être seul pour penser que les empereurs
de la Chine avaient les ongles très longs.
Ça les empêchait de faire un poing.
Ils n'avaient pas besoin d'en faire, peut-être.
On laisse ça aux paysans. Quand on est
empereur, il faut avoir de la dignité.
On apprécie les oiseaux sans les imiter.
On connait bien cheval, éléphant, ministre, fourmi.
Les poings, on s'en fout. Cela manque d'élégance.

Certains disent que la chose difficile
en écrivant, c'est de commencer.
Ceci dit . . . . il n'y a plus de difficulté,
théoriquement, au moins. Le premier mot est déjà prononcé.
Et, parlant théorie, j'en ai une.
(Hypocrite hypothèse, mon semblable, mon frère) :
Les mots sur la page
Deviennent des otages
Et parlant d'Iran
Ils n'iront pas loin.
Mais dès que tu oses
écrire quelque chose
Il n'y a plus de peur :
Voilà le bonheur !

Written October 1981, before Shambhala Training, Level One

Dear Notebook, listen to me!

I have to say,
if only to see where it leads,
some things which won't bother anyone.

Humid night. Children all in bed.
Thanks to the absence of harsh critics,
I dare to speak. First of all, I remember
a striking thought:
I take delight in it at this very moment.
Yes, precious solitude, it is you
I am talking about, after all, you have to
be alone to think that the Emperors
of China had very long nails.
It stopped them from making a fist.
They had no need to, perhaps.
That can be left to the peasants.
To be an emperor requires dignity.
You appreciate birds without imitating them.
You know all about horse, elephant, minister, ant.
You could care less about fists. They lack elegance.

Some people say that what's hard
about writing is starting.
That having been said . . . . there is no more difficulty,
theoretically, at least. The first word has already been spoken.
And, speaking of theory, I've got one for you.
(Hypocritical hypothesis, my fellow, my brother):
The words on the pages
Become hostages
And speaking of Iran
They won't go far.
But as soon as you dare
put something in writing
There is no more fear:
There's happiness for you!

Translated from the French by Kunga Dawa and Claire Broughton.

Don't rain on my tirade

The feeling is upon me
to write without forethought
whatever comes to mind,
an unpremeditated sortie
into flow of consciousness,
a dyptych, a doodle bug,
a pure bold joyous tirade in the face of
wind and weather and poor memory.
My only concern shall be
to let go, let flow, without the least inhibition.
OOOOH. Now what does that bring?
Pictures of lovely brown-eyed woman
with delicious breasts, long hair like spun silk
and luscious full lips, made for kissing?
Certainly not, knot tied with strong string,
hard to disentangle. The cobweb of desire?

What, then? A peevish tirade
against the right wing, wrong wing,
four flushing double dealing liars
that have trampled and shredded
all that's valuable in this dear country?
You know of whom I speak, friend.
Surely no need to name them.
Those that have dragged us into
costly war under false pretenses,
the same that shamelessly rob the poor and hungry
to heap more wealth upon the richest few,
are turning America into fascist country, brutal police state;
those that willingly undo the few remaining laws
that protect land, water and air
to profit insatiable greed of corporate backers.
Only to-day a neighbor and friend, Aaron Kuykendal,
bet me $5:00 that there won't even be a presidential election

in the coming year. And I shaking on it, saying,
*sure, they'll try to steal it, like they did the last one,
but at least they'll pretend to hold a fair and free election.*
But will they, though?
Am I the gullible fool to think so?

What is it best to do in these wretched times
when all our values are turned upside down
by the criminals in power?
And freedom, justice and compassion—
those precious imponderables,
vanishing like the morning mist?
(Ah, Lulu. Your real name, I'm told,
is Hallelujah Mist-on-the-Mountains.)
Become an activist, war protester,
supporter of MoveOn.org?
Cry out against nuclear proliferation,
Los Alamos a *la mode,*
(no nukes is good nukes)?
Oppose the Homeland Insecurity
the black hand of repression
armed with tazer guns, rubber bullets
and plastic handcuffs to bind
and gag those who would raise
their voices in peaceful protest?
Or rather...
stay in retreat and focus all effort
on enlightenment? Or giving up
even the hope of that: Just stay
unmoved in the state of nondual awareness?
And come out just occasionally
to share the dharma with others,
point the way to self-liberation,
as civil liberties go down the drain?

Perplexing questions.
And lifespan is limited,
am growing day by day
closer to closure, to naked death
to give its true name. The end
of this life. Better make the best of it, then.
Not waste what's left. Get your book or two
written, if you can. Legacy to leave behind.
Pass on naked when done to whatever
follows after: a form of being
disembodied for a while?
And a chance, maybe,
to reflect on the life that's past?
(No time to re-write the script.)
And leaving what behind?
A little book of poems—
a handful only?
A quickly fading memory
in the minds of three sons
and a handful of friends?
Did I create something
or add some thing of value
to this sweet blue planet?
Or will I have frittered away
this precious life in doodling
and dabbling, bound in the chains
of small pleasures, cowardly evasions,
too little achieved?
AH. It's achievement you want, is it?
Better throw that one out the window too.
It stinks like a piece of shit
wrapped in brocade.
Just stick to what small things are

true, kind and decent.
Can you manage that, now,
while breath still comes and goes?

And give thanks
for sick cyclamen
that has revived,
for petunias
that still flower in winter,
for breath that does still flow,
for tabby kitten name of Scooter
who only asks to rub his nose
against mine and teach me
how to purr. The teaching of
the Great Purrfection.
I'm workin' on it, Scoots.
Apurr-ciate. Apurr-ciate.
That's it, that's it.
It's coming to me now!

    Thanksgiving day, 2003

Gratitude

You are the plump pigeon in Trafalgar Square
perching briefly on Lord Nelson's shoulder,
you are the fountain too, with its generous
jet of cool water to delight the senses.

You are the holy hall of mirrors
in the elevator of La Fonda Hotel
in Santa Fe, reflecting perfectly
all who go up and come down
with your inscrutable third eye.

You are the dark haired dakini,
the one who cried in the salon
after the careless cutter took
too much of your black hair

leaving you sadly shorn.
Or was it Sean who left you, sadly,
after you discovered him, presciently,
in the bakery drinking his coffee

with another sangha girl,
the faithless treacherous man?
You are the sunrise over the Bay,
the red wine in the crystal goblet,

the one who loves poetry,
carries Mary Oliver in her back pack,
the one whom poets can't help loving,
the spreading young ivy's luxuriant growth
that clings to the wall of our imagining,

the apple blossom and corn fields of Iowa,
the rightful inheritor, if truth be told,
of a fine log cabin in California hills
stolen away by deceitful treachery.

You are the note left in Nissan truck
with bar of rich dark mocha chocolate
and the warmth of a woven red shawl.
You are the sound of African salsa

that mingles inextricably
with the rhythmic heartbeat
of grey-haired poet in adobe cabin
in northern New Mexico,

capturing bright butterfly words
to pin them on the page,
their wings still fluttering
with inextricable gratitude.
Merci, chère amie, merci!

Kyoto in Autumn

Kyoto in autumn:
Was it the girl's sad smile
or that perfect maple tree
by the temple gate
that broke my heart?

La Grande Illusion

Security. You think you have it
and it vanishes like puff of smoke.
Think of the finest coat you ever owned
how you looked good in it
how it kept you warm a winter night,
cashmere it may have been
or camel hair lined with silk
and good deep pockets to put your hands in.
Where is it now? Gone, all gone.
The lovely woman who wore your ring
who swore she loved you
walked with you hand in hand
through East Village wearing
white sheepskin coat, a touch
of Rive Gauche by Yves Saint Laurent,
arched her back to meet you
or gripped you with her dancer's thighs
on New York steamy nights.
Where is she now?
Far away in another country
eating ramen noodles
in a tiny apartment,
a grandma wrinkled with
bad teeth and bitter memories
righteous anger at the wrongful world.

My own golden youth:
the dancing in river beds
Ibiza in a cloud of hashish
the careless acid trips in Central Park
giggling and goggling at
marble pillars in Plaza Hotel
wide-eyed and paranoid
when asked to leave by house detective.
Staying up all night in Max's Kansas City

or Village Vanguard to dig
the wailing weaving sounds
of Rahsaan Roland Kirk,
saxaphone genius with wild array of horns
blowing incendiary bright moments
the rip rig and panic of blind jazzman's
search for searing truth, why don't they know?
All vanished long ago.
Rahsaan dead and gone
these thirty years.

And this still living breathing
fool for love, greyhaired now,
sits alone in adobe cabin
in high desert of New Mexico
listening to the falling snow
melting, dripping off the roof,
feeding pinon logs
into old woodstove,
kept warm chiefly by
rhythmic rich harmonies
of Coleman Hawkins
Duke Ellington
Manu Dibango,
nothing much to hold onto
at last. A breath of music,
bright moon rise,
whatever comes and goes
as all things must.
Learning finally to . . .
let go
let go
let go,
laisser tomber
finalement
la grande illusion.

Louisiana Party Pick-Up

Soul Sister, do play New Orleans hot jazz
Tabasco music cookin' sweet an' wild.
Southern watermelon boy want it again
As fancy French Quarter dude is eatin' Peggy Sue.
Gonna chew Dixie belle's spicy crawfish can
Fishin' in her slick mission love hash,
Goin' down on Georgia girl's fantastic hospitality possum
Creole cowboy can rise poker hard in rude union
Or politely say, "Fair lady, ifnya take my piggly wiggly
We will git happy together rasslin
'til the very Mississippi knows
How beautiful our dirty dancin' is."

*This poem was composed in New Orleans using a fridge magnet set with *Southern* vocabulary.

Dog Day Blues

Dog goes to his bowl,
why's he feeling so blue?
The bowl being empty
he starts on my shoe.
He rips off the upper,
what a song is being sung!
Yes, he'll sing for his supper
now that he's got the tongue.
Giving voice to his joy
just like Nat King Cole,
he is such a bad boy
but he surely has sole . . .

No Regret

I have no regret.
True, I was drunk
was drunk with Diane
drank the wine of her
tasted her flesh
her deepest place
intoxicated, the sweet
and salty wine of her,
drunk with love,
believing I could
ride the waves,
the great waves
of desire insatiable,
like a young beach boy,
a California surfer
riding the tunnel triumphant.

When at last the wave
broke and crashed
and dragged me under
oh, I came close,
came close to drowning
swallowing salt tears,
close to drowning,
thrown lifeless at last
on the lonely beach.
Bruised ribs,
hands full of sand
and the taste of her yet
in my mouth.

I have no regret,
to go deep,
to have loved, perhaps,
beyond my means,
spent all and no regret, and
the seagull's harsh cry calling
calling me back
to the deep and lovely ocean
with its white-capped waves,
calling, calling me back
to the lovely ocean,
deep and deadly,
the siren call.

Plunge deep,
drown if you must,
or sit on beach and watch
the endless, the endless procession
of waves rolling in.
Or sit on beach
and know the time
has not yet come
for you to die.

What if I take the Jewel Lake pills?

I got to read more poetry
write more poems
stay alive a while yet
take Tibetan medicine.
They say the Rinchen Tso
Jewel Lake pills
taken only on full moon
after fasting and no sex
actually reverse
the aging process.

Hello youngsters!
here I come
back from one-foot-in-the-grave
to who knows what
youthful indiscretions.
Will I end up
making love to sweet
young Buddhist woman
with tender hungry mouth
and gila monster tattooed
on her pretty ass?
She says it's the only thing
Keeps her from being enlightened.
What does *she* know?

Eight nights ago
we circumnavigated
the Great Stupa of Dharmakaya
by moonlight in a red Nissan 200SX
and made great aspiration
to attain buddhahood
for the sake of holy north America.

Now she's off to spend a couple days
with her high school sweetheart
in Carbondale, Colorado.
She said she fell in love
With his hands, for god's sake,
Back when she was seventeen.

After we kissed she sighed
And said, *let's not*
Ruin a good friendship.
While we were kissing
She laughed:
Funny to be kissin'
Someone old enough
To be your dad.

She called her father
for a plane ticket to Canada
instead of going back to school.
Wants to live at Gampo Abbey
maybe shave her head
become a nun.
The folks at the Abbey
told her maybe she should
go back to school after all,
but if not, then pack a bag
and come up to Cape Breton
in October. What would you do?
What will I do?
Grow young in Boulder
selling Subarus to upwardly mobile?
Or do long retreat in New Mexico
and practice the teachings
of the Great Perfection
gazing at the sky by day

and checking out
the sparkling light of darkness
taking Bardo as the path by night?

The path is lonely
and I might as well
travel it that way.
Little likelihood of marrying again.
The only one I'd want to marry
is the crazy wisdom dakini lady
with the dark hair and blue-green eyes
whose name I dare not mention.
She told me specifically
to leave her out of my poems
from now on, and here she comes,
sneaking back into one of them
incognito, the only way to go.

Remember sitting on her bed
and holding hands
to the African sounds
of Foday Musa Suso
and talking about
exploring the boundaries of Mind,
her skin so smooth
there were no boundaries
that I remember.

That was the last time
I saw her and honestly
don't know when
I'll see her agin.
Probably not until
then next time I close
my eyes while Oliver Nelson

plays Stolen Moments
and thunder rolls
in the Colorado sky
Around Midnight.

And that night we promised
whichever one of us
attained enlightenment first
would come back and help the other
over the hump over the bump
bopping and bouncing
down the bumpy road to buddhahood
in Boulder, Colorado, now this minute
resting in the natural state
tracking down the minute particulars
of sacred nowness at midnight
under a diamond-studded sky.

Summer Lightning

In southern sky
summer lightning
ripples and flickers
just like close
encounters of the third
kind. I gave you
a ride from town
to Three Rocks
lovely young hitch-hiker
of the galaxy
the warmth of your hand
in mine awakens memory

Chance encounter
with warm skin
unfettered breasts
considering brown eyes
so young and yet so wise.
You told me
*"I like some loving
in the morning."*

Will I ever
awaken at 6:00 AM
with your arms around me
and lose my way
in your lazy kisses
erect nipples
(summer lightning
flickers and ripples)
smooth belly breathing me in
as the sun's fire burns away all trace
of the dark night place
where I lay alone?

Particles and galaxies collide
when lips and tongue meet
and your hands guide
my strong bone sweet
to your liquid center
drawing me in
wave upon wave
in the southern sky
to a fiery grave
melting us down
with a deep sigh
just a ride from town.

When I have to die
will it be like this
in your strong embrace
with a loving kiss?
Or shall I rather
as I grow older
wrap the cloak of solitude
around my shoulder
and when this life's trajectory
has spent its force,
laying down on my right side
the way the Buddha died,
shall I release my spirit
from this cage of bones
with filaments of light
to guide its course
back to the formless
original source
from which I came
to planet earth
when I made the choice
to take a human birth?

Song of Dependent Origination

—for Allen Ginsberg

At age 20 I first read HOWL and a tremor ran through underground student union potsmoke
acid-test Beatle brewed cities from Newcastle to London to Paris and back.
Oh shock of recognition and Baudelairean ecstasy, hearing the true and vibrant
voice of America not to go unheard by this sick sad planet.
In 1961 at Byre Theatre in St. Andrews, Scotland, I read Beat poems at midnight
to stunned excited audience. Xmas teeth! They loved it and howled for more,
though heaven knows it wasn't exactly the best minds of my generation saved by sanity.
Traveling with Chogyam Trungpa to India in 1968 in Benares by holy Ganges
we encountered crazed and awe-struck hippy pilgrim pointing to the very spot—
right here, man, see—
where Allen Ginsberg and Peter Orlovsky got stoned with the sadhus.
At sacred cave of Paro Tagtsang in Bhutan saw vision of New York skyline
and knew that I would come to north America, and came choiceless to New York
blown by wind of karma in 1970, year of Kent State massacre Black Panther riots
while Trungpa came to Montreal apartment adorned with poster of Einstein
and you, Allen, sporting stars and stripes and sandwich board of legalize pot.
That summer on burning Manhattan sidewalk outside Museum of Modern Art samurai movie
black-bearded poet in a hurry, you stole our taxi, Allen the famous cab-thief rushing.
Two days later you came to meet Trungpa Rinpoche at Dawn's 5th floor walk-up lower
East Side apartment and we chanted—or rather sang —the Sadhana of Mahamudra
harmoniumized with chords.

March of 73 you gave me The Fall of America inscribed
"For Kunga Dawa, dirty liar in thanks for lies,
Bodhisattva Compassion to my suffering sweat, Love Allen Ginsberg. AH."
Link in chain of ten-things-lead-to-another—pratityasamutpada—and who knows what
occasional karmic encounters at TV studios and Dharma gatherings across America.
Now ten more years have passed and we are somewhat slowed down fellow travelers
on Dharma and Shambhala path. You have become Bodhisattva bard
who gave meditation instruction to Chinese interpreter,
gentler by far than what you were, shinjanged, patient and generous beyond belief
to Naropa students and assorted Dharma bums from Boulder to Bangkok,

from Beijing to New Delhi traveling electric neon poetry highways from minarets of
Moscow to Prague to Istanbul, Rome, London, New York, San Francisco
legacy of Blake and Whitman visionary cocksucker poet for this suffering planet.
Another decade slips away and last night in Alfalfa's grocery apparently by chance
we met again—one more link in the cosmic karmic chain of auspicious coincidence.
You had bags of fresh vegetables, more than you could carry,
and I was able to be your taxi driver, watch while you cut up leeks with practiced hand,
listen while you praised the leafy carrot tops, chopped them into your stainless-steel cauldron,
Allen the alchemist, stirring life-enhancing soup, organic ingredients, macrobiotic,
big life, big fish in Naropa pond, grain of sand in big universe, proud pedophiliac,
impossible hide under bed, humble practitioner, always good friend.

Welcome back, Allen,
welcome Dharma brother,
writing whatever needs to be written,
teaching whatever needs to be taught,
singing whatever needs to be sung
without doubt. AH AH AH

for Allen Ginsberg, clean soothsayer, with thanks forsooth.

Sunshine Angel

Brown-eyed greencard angel in cowboy boots and faded jeans
couldn't wait to leave home at fifteen praying in teenage bed come America
escape Catholic family subservient female role-play nothing new in Noves
free to be your own self in US leaving Provence for Providence Rhode Island
au pair girl look after three year old boy for college professor family
take greyhound bus to Boulder, Colorado, Rocky Mountain playground,
American people so kind everywhere smoke grass New Orleans for Mardi Gras—
What's a nice girl like you doing here?—crashing at Head Inn,
taking hallucinogenic mushrooms peyote acid trip and hashish,
sleeping bags in hallway 50 cents per day don't wanna go back to France.

Why did I dream of you that night after Buddha talk at Taos library
to understand your spirit of sunshine wisdom angel name?
What message your knowing eyes hold and long boned healing hands?
Maturity hard-earned after vegetarian wanderings traveling light
and gave away your power to fake guru, yet in a vision received
blessing from authentic vajra master Kalu Rinpoche
offering encouragement follow your heart's true path
and now you practice daily meditation
taught by Vietnamese monk and master healer,
give thanks for great bodhisattvas able radiate peace, compassion:

Thich Nhat Han and H.H. Dalai Lama whose religion is kindness
selfless empty mind interbeing connectedness of every leaf and tree
and footfall awakened heart bodhicitta caring for all beings everywhere
including America death-machine Pentagon overkill
GI Joe massacres at My Lai and a thousand villages—
women with babies slaughtered from helicopter gun ships
young girl ablaze with napalm jelly screaming down the death road
two million killed in south-east Asia all for what?

Avalokita's forgiveness too for China's Red Army genocide
liberating Tibetans from a thousand years of Dharma practice
six thousand monasteries reduced to rubble
monks and nuns forced to copulate at gunpoint
old man's thumbs hacked off for telling mantra beads
Om Mani Padme Hum sacred syllables of compassion
lamas imprisoned beaten tortured starved
cattle-prod burns on brown flesh twenty years or more
women forcibly sterilized refugees fleeing by night on foot
stumbling through deep snow over treacherous mountain passes
the strong the few reaching at last the kingdom of Nepal
or holy mother India cradle of the Buddha Dharma
maybe trek to Dharmsala home of Tenzin Gyatso, Kundun,
winner of Nobel peace prize never giving up on sentient beings,
merci. With gratitude you think of them.

And yes, you need to eat buffalo meat from Cid's now
reclaim your strength and spirit firm under Taos mountain
offer energy balancing intuitive healing comes from universe
giving what's needed naturally free clinic Mondays
but you've earned the right to stable home
make money for good cause visit daughter in Atlanta
Titania in school play fairy queen fly her here
for Spring break she does still need you,
Even your ex understands that.

You have dreamed again and again of taureaux, taureaux,
taureaux, stampeding through narrow sunbaked streets of Avignon
with white horns sharpened while you lie down flat
arms stretched wide in surrender, dream hooves passing over you harmless,
the need to understand finally the intricate steps of male/female dance,
untangling the tango of sun and moon, yin and yang, yabyum,
sleeping peacefully in bright light big sky studio on Camino del Medio.
May it come to pass as you wish, sunshine angel!

Nothing Wanting

Sweetie, since you asked, there's nothing,
nothing that I want from you,
nothing needed, nothing wanting,
everything's complete and perfect
just the way it is. It cannot
be improved upon nor
made less in any way:
estoy contento, mi amor.

True, the golden memories
of all we shared: the glorious
mountain hikes and sitting
on rock beside the trail
to catch our breath,
and Bald Mountain
with the breathless view
out over the plains
and the world's perfect
roundness clearly seen;

fine meals in sunny courtyard
of the Med, lamb meatballs
in sherry and cilantro, fresh
calamata olive bread
dipped in olive oil
and aged balsamic;
the way you hated it
when I talked with friendly
smile to waitresses,
treating them as friends
and calling them by name:

all are stored in the crystal
archive of selective memory,
brightly vivid like fragrant petals
from the roses I delivered
to Zen Center for your birthday.

Sitting together, sharing
meditation and dharma path,
taking delight in studying
the *when which how* practice
of *living from the heart*;

your perfect breasts, the lovely kisses,
sweet caresses and orgasmic sighs,
the sheer joy and wonder of it;
the times you panicked
and bolted and I not knowing
if you'd come back
and happy when you did;
growing, learning little by little,
even in the face of
too often broken words.

And thanks, dear heart,
for talking last night
on the phone with
such kindness and candor,
helping me to see it was largely
my own stubborn mountain goat tenacity,
insisting too much on *what I wanted*,
not giving you the space
to freely honor *your* commitments,
that made it hard for you
to stay the course with me.

It is never easy to see
one's own faults, alas.
Enabling me to see mine
more clearly is a priceless gift,
one that I will value highly
and learn from, so that,
when the time comes,
I will tread a little lighter
in the tango of what
love may come next time.
Bless you for that, dear friend!

And now, in truth, there's nothing,
nothing more I want from you;
nothing wanting, everything complete.
If you were to go
down Federal Boulevard
to Alameda and find
a Chinese cup to replace
the one of mine you broke,
in a destructive act,
it would only be for you
to make amends, and not for me.
There's nothing that I need and
nothing that I want from you,
at last, dieu merci.
May we both be free!

Feb 8, 2009

Magnetic

I dream of cool moon-shine bed,
lazy tongue to smooth white breast
languidly lusting for sweet bare skin.
Let me lie in your peach petal garden
and swim easy in your timeless love lake.
I need you to rock me lightly,
whisper like drunk woman and,
after my purple ache is gone,
I will say, *we did it, honey girl.*

*The words for this poem were selected from a fridge magnet set. Hence the double *entendre* of the title.

Doubtful Katheryn

*Dixit: sed mulier cupido quod dixit amanti
In vento et rapida scribere opportet aqua.* (Catullus)*

**She said: but what a woman says to a passionate lover
should be written in the wind and the raging torrents.*

And what did I expect, if anything?
Did not Francois, the noble king
with his peerless diamond ring
write on the prison window pane
"Souvent femme varie"?
Often—oh often—woman is changeable.
See how her feelings come and go
like the fitful breeze of Spring,
she'll come and go like anything.
One day it's *Oh, my darling,
I love you so very much.*
The next day, like a starling
or busy little thrush,
she's building a *new* nest
because just *now* that's what feels best.

Gazing with her clear blue eyes,
Katheryn can epitomize
the brilliant words of William Blake,
which I will quote for my own sake:
"He who binds to himself a joy
does the winged life destroy,
but he who kisses the joy as it flies
lives in eternity's sunrise."

I'll heed the wisdom of these words
and give my love to *all* the birds
who freely fly and sing their songs
untroubled by man's "rights and wrongs."
I will live fully in the here and now,
be faithful to my heartfelt vow
to love all beings without exception
and speak my truth with no deception.

Yet still I love sweet Katie Sue,
my constant heart is free from doubt.
To you I always will be true:
I know what true love's all about.
It doesn't waver, come and go,
but pulses with a steady glow
that reaches out to everyone
with timeless radiance, like the sun.

Beaucoup Haiku for Katie Sue

Please let your hair down.
Seeing you so tall and lovely,
I just let go of everything.

    Dharma bones are empty.
    Yet still they rattle around
    inside this grateful body.

        Taking silverware
        to the nun Jin Hai,
        I carefully forget the knives.

            Can you take me to urgent care?
            After reading this letter from her,
            I think I've got a broken heart.

                Did you say the flame of love?
                It's just Dakini Kate
                burning up my stuff.

Sonnetry confinement

A single month has passed since first we met
and from my window watched the full moon rise.
I did not mean to fall in love, and yet
something about you took me by surprise.
My mind was captured by your quirky smile,
your bright brown eyes, their warmth, your inner strength.
I fought these strange emotions for while
but daily love grew stronger, and at length
the depth of feeling could not be denied.
Did I do wrong to tell you how I feel?
Should I have kept it bottled up inside?
Now you avoid me, stand me up, reveal
a cruel indifference, while my only sin
is caring for you deeply, dearest Lynn.

Zozobra

Old Man Gloom
fifty feet high
with a black bow tie
groans and starts to turn
his marionette head.
"Let him burn let him burn,"
a thousand voices cry
and he knows he'll soon be dead.

In his ghostly entrail
my own sad thoughts are written:
my son's in jail,
and my girlfriend's quittin'.
At last it's my turn
to watch the sorrows burn,
release the pointless blames
(may they all go up in flames)
and I'll live a little lighter
remembering their names.

Thursday, September 6th, 2007
Gates Open At 2:00 P.M.
Entertainment Begins at 3:35 P.M.
Burning At Dusk, Rain or Shine

The white page is an invitation

The white page is an invitation.
I will travel gladly between its lines
so full of promise, guiding my boat,
the wellspring of my creativity,
along the smooth canal. For my
hearing aid, I'll listen to that soft
inner voice that has its own way
of speaking, gentle but insistent,
and record its messages in the hear and now,
unhesitatingly, for the sake of those who,
in the future, after my death, will hear or read
these words.

Listeners and readers, I offer you
my heart and blood and bones. I call down
a radiant shower of blessings upon you.
I offer you the timbre and resonance of my voice,
let it echo down the years, let it speak to your hearts,
let it be as though I stand before you,
naked and confident, as the light
from the center of my rib cage shines out,
as the warmth of my hands
touches and quickens you, as we look
into each other's eyes
and at this moment recognize
our deep kinship, which time
does nothing to erase.

Those who have lived and held power
at the time these words were written
caused great harm to our beautiful planet
in our name, always in our name.
And yet the light carriers, the network
of committed souls incarnate, all who practice
the heart's intelligence of limitless love,

choose to be filaments of coherent energy
to weave the brilliant and ever-shifting tapestry
of planetary evolution, and for this
I reach out my skeletal arms, my hollow
pulsing hands in gratitude and joyous welcome:
knowing for sure: the earth shall shine anew
and those of us who care, who deeply care,
will soon return to quicken and heal
this sweet blue planet once again. So be it!

Song for Dakini Kate

Play with PlayDough,
Fight with Fredo,
Down a dozen beers.
At any rate, be truly Kate
And rise above your fears.

You've got the goods,
You love the woods,
You know your natural home.
To be quite true, all I can do
is offer you this poem.

You've won my heart.
When we're apart
I miss you very much.
I kiss your eyes and realize
I need your loving touch.

You're tall and strong
And all along
I've loved you since we met.
So hand in hand let's roam this land
And pay our karmic debt.

Resolution

I wanna write more
I'm gonna do it too
d'une facon journaliere
only way to go.

Will take some lifestyle
changes, que no?
Fewer movie rentals
forget Netflix.

Just a notebook
and pen poised,
a willingness to start
from the shining moment,

to spill the guts
of whatever arises,
the green pears
in their white bowl,

the trembling
luminous water drops
on patio cross beam,
the odd head lines
in Union Tribune:

Nirvana for Dog Show,
Schottenheimer axed by Chargers,
Stone Age Chimps Used Tools.
What does it all mean?

It doesn't matter much.
Just look and see,
record the vibrant moment
in all its quirky glory
and share the song with
whoever come who may.

Storm before the war

Big snow storm
wind strong from north
try lighting leaky woodstove:
icy backdraft and smoke
smoke smoke filling
cabin—choke choke choke,
cough and blast it!
Windows open and
cold cold air mingling
with choky smoky.
Hack hack—can't
hack it. Give up,
stop being obstinate fool.
Take blanket, bag of food,
Time to go find
shelter at friend's house.

Necessity is the great
mother, tap you on the shoulder
kind, better listen to me
go quietly into that
snow blowing night,
visit friend sleep couch
her cigarette smoke
not as bad as wood stove
backdraft smoke inhalation
nightmare in freezing
hilltop cabin. So . . .
relax. Phone White House
tell Bush cancel war.
How many thousands
children in Iraq
not our enemies
will be killed
maimed by US bombs?

We value life?
C'mon George,
Get a grip.
Shock and Awe?
3,000 deadly missiles
on Basra and Baghdad?
*"A form of terrorism
of the very worst kind,"*
Dennis Halliday calls it.

May the satellite
that guides the missiles
fall to earth, tanks
get lost in sandstorm,
American people rise up
say no to war
recall the troops,
regain our sanity.
It's about time,
isn't it?

The Blessed of my life

The first day of the blessed of my life!
And it's 88 degrees and a slight breeze
waving the petunias, white and magenta,
my son Mike drinking Tequiza and watering his little pot seed,
waiting for it to bud up with spiky green leaves ready to roll.
But he'll be back in Toronto by then
and what'll I do with the silly weed?
Let Serafina eat it maybe,
that sweet calico kitty with super sharp teeth?
Sometimes she likes to climb up my jeans.
Claws'll grab onto anything
and she's a climber, I'm tellin' ya.

We ate Pad Thai Noodles for lunch
with chicken and cilantro and napa cabbage.
When I look to the sky, dancing twirling
dots appear against hot white clouds.
Some insect got to my left foot
when I went out to pee from the deck
—no-see'um or pesky skeeter. Red and itchy on top.
I'll apply some a' that Pearl Essential Balm
to ease the itch so I can hear again
that slow steady inner music, audible only
in the scented silence of this high mesa
stretching far to the south, a sea of sage brush
from here to the Three Peaks and beyond,
the Sangre de Cristo mountains
lazy hazy blue on the far horizon.
Don't fence me in ... Inner space
mingling with hot blue sky,
bunch a' little cotton wool clouds
floatin' up there over Wheeler Peak to the east.

Sip tea and write for the joy of it.
The hot world spins as it pleases.
And to-day I'll let it and watch it
and offer up some soup from my bones and marrow
as a pleasing gift for insatiable beings.
May their craving be quelled and minds be at ease.
I'll ride to Taos in old blue Subaru,
order healing herbs for Mike and me
and share the ephemeral gift of poetry
with young slammers at the Southside Bean.
Riding the hot wind easy as it blows
listening for its wake-up call in the piñon trees:
the natural prayer rising from the prairies.

Them Apples

Ah, those uncanny celebratory apples
    the gala beauties crisp sweet and rosy-cheeked
        as any spring time girl
            running in cold morning air
                her breath a quick small cloud
                    dissolving like a brief desire
                      shall we offer you to the awakened ones
                    or plant a seed of you
                in nutrient earth in early march
              water it tenderly as any ma
            and watch with pride the first fine shoots
        of you perk up and open perfect
    green leaves to the ever-renewing
blessed sol that warms the grateful earth?

why not do this instead
    of making needless heedless children
        to furrow your brows
            stain your cheeks with salt rivulets
                exhaust all your endeavours
                    diverting you from dharma path
                      aging you swiftly with toil and care?
                  Are there not stakes enough
              in this carnivorous world
            and did not Guru Padma say
        "Children may be very lovely
    but they're the stakes
that bind you to samsara"?

why not adopt instead
    the way of Shantideva
        the way the sufi saint Raihana Mataji
            taught me in New Delhi
                her door ever open to come who may:
                    regard all beings depending on their age
                    as mothers fathers brothers sisters
                    daughters sons, honoring our kinship
                through life after life
           embracing all with knowledge that
        as the Mayans have it
in lakech—I am another yourself?

Things to Remember

Mail card to Veronique in Boulder
thanks your kind offer. May I stay your house
March 9th and 10th on Timber Lane?
Watch breath go out dissolve
become breath, mingling mind and sky
Send postcard to Julian in Tampa
got your message, sure, but how come your phone
is disco, no longer in service, huh?
Impossible visit that way please write
I wanna come meet Jade, that girl's
gotta right to know her grandpa.
Recognize rigpa let go of thoughts
C'mon now, just remember, right?
Bring notes, toothpaste, shave cream, marmalade
sports coat, clean socks, Leanna's phone number
meet her Friday Dominic café for lunch 11:45
blind date with Jungian analyst, slim, blond
good-looking (her own estimate) catching plane later
take shower, wear clean shirt, make good impression?
Come back to breath, expand, dissolve, disown.
Leave food for Kitty, check oil
get spark plugs Autozone, oil change soon
check weather forecast or look sky
see snow clouds coming cancel trip stay home.
Ah, no. Can't do that. Remember,
level II, Birth of Warrior?
breathe out, breathe in, breathe out.
Put out remains of bok choy cabbage,
some parts still good, for rabbits.
breathe out, expand, let be, disown
Aha! That's it, slow down now
take it easy. Relax, breathe out, expand.
merge mind and space, let go.
not follow thought look into thinker
look into Mastercard zero interest thru' July

zero degrees break ice on cistern
send in truck registration renewal
renew, come back, come back to now
label with light touch, mmm hmm
just touch and go, mmm hmm
expand, dissolve Aha!
light touch fresh air let go,
remember?
Ah Ah Ah
remember?
Ah Ah Ah

Feb. 4, 2004

The elephants in your wallet

—*for Erik Pema Kunsang*

May the elephants in your wallet copulate thunderously and present you with many gifted offspring;
May Vaishravana and Jambhala party hearty in your apartments and shower you with lakhs of rupees;
May the haughty milk-babe's mongoose vomit glittering diamonds, rubies, emeralds, sapphires (who needs topaz?), overflowing your alabaster chamber pots with magnificence;
May your favorite servant graduate *summa cum laude* from Cordon Bleu and astound you with gourmet delights
every time she announces, with her humble knock, "M'sieur, Dame, le diner est servi"
and dinner guests will throw down their silver forks in amazement, exclaiming, *Your didi didn' do dat, did she? 'Ome sweet Om, Shanti!*
May your marital coupling send shock waves of empty bliss through your avadhuti
'til the corridors of Ka Nying Shedrup Ling are glowing with pulsing rainbows and even Chöling is cheering;
May the merit of your peerless translations gain global recognition, Pullitzer prizes, Nobel laurels for literature
- Oh, the banquets in Stockholm: the Dane done did it dis time – and hordes of haughty Duffs are humbled in your dust,
while the profound Dharma spreads through the known and unknown universe, delighting the lineage gurus.
May the viciousness of your peerless consort slash the aorta of somnolence and ever keep you on your toes,
dancing with defenseless ease graceful minuets, tangoes and OM PAPA, OOM PAPA waltzes.
May the snakespit concoctions of Wagnerian sorcerer cure whatever ails you and bring your body to previously unknown pitch of perfect health.
May your fabled excellence and renown be celebrated by expat British pigtailed poet 'til the whole wide world salutes you, acknowledging the king of translators!

Book summary

The poems collected here span 1980 – 2010. Putting this book together was a labor of love and many contributed to make it possible: Paul Seaton suggested it, Lois Silverstein recommended Xlibris.

Special thanks to my guru, Chogyam Trungpa, who said, *"All my students are artists. Some just don't know it yet;"* to Allen Ginsberg, poetry mentor in early 90's: to the following whose generous help was indispensable: David Bolduc, Sarah Morelli, Liz Crow, Aaron Goldstein, Claire Broughton and, not least, Katheryn Miller who inspired so much. I love and thank you all.

About the Author

Richard Arthure, better known by his Buddhist name, Kunga Dawa (All-Joyful Moon), was a close student of Chögyam Trungpa Rinpoche and was the first Westerner authorized by him to teach the Dharma.

He has traveled and taught extensively throughout the US, Canada and Europe, transmitting the Buddhist and Shambhala teachings with characteristic insight and humor.

Richard now makes his home in Boulder, Colorado, where he gives occasional poetry readings, rides his bike, drinks a lot of tea, and continues to relate to students.